# SUPPOSING HIM TO BE THE GARDENER

# Metropolitan Tabernacle Pulpit.

# SUPPOSING HIM TO BE THE GARDENER

## A Sermon

Delivered on Lord's Day Morning,
December 31ST, 1882, by

## Charles H. Spurgeon

at the Metropolitan Tabernacle, Newington.

Updated to modern language by Charles J. Doe

Minneapolis

Published by Curiosmith.
Minneapolis, Minnesota.
Internet: curiosmith.com.

Previously published by PASSMORE & ALBASTER.

The text of this edition is from the *Metropolitan Tabernacle Pulpit*, Volume 29, Sermon 1699.

The text was updated to modern equivalents of Elizabethan and Victorian words and phrases. Occasional occurrences of lengthy sentences and close punctuation were left unchanged.

Scripture quotations designated (NIV) are from the Holy Bible, NEW INTERNATIONAL VERSION®. Copyright © 1973, 1978, 1984 by Biblica, Inc. All rights reserved worldwide. Used by permission.

Definitions are from Webster's Revised Unabridged Dictionary, 1828 and 1913.

The "Guide to the Contents" was added to this edition by the publisher.

Modern language text, supplementary content, and cover design: Copyright © 2014 Charles J. Doe.

ISBN 9781941281161

## *GUIDE TO THE CONTENTS*

INTRODUCTION. Jesus Christ is the gardener. (PAGE 7)

I. THE KEY TO MANY WONDERS. (PAGE 11)
    A. The wonder that there should be a church at all in the world. (PAGE 11)
    B. The wonder that the church of God came to flourish in such a climate. (PAGE 12)
    C. The wonder that we should ever have been placed among the plants of the Lord. (PAGE 14)
    D. The wonder that evils have been shut out for so long a time. (PAGE 15)

II. A SPUR TO MANY DUTIES. (PAGE 16)
    A. The duty of a Christian is joy. (PAGE 16)
    B. The duty of valuing the Lord's presence and praying for it. (PAGE 18)
    C. The duty to yield oneself up entirely to Christ. (PAGE 19)
    D. The duty to bring forth fruit to Christ. (PAGE 20)

III. A RELIEF FROM CRUSHING RESPONSIBILITY. (PAGE 22)
    A. A relief from excessive care about prosperity. (PAGE 22)
    B. A relief from keeping all the church in order. (PAGE 22)
    C. A relief to not question the wisdom of my task. (PAGE 24)
    D. A relief from cases which are extremely difficult. (PAGE 24)
    E. A relief from having so many plants to look after that we have not time to cultivate any one. (PAGE 25)
    F. A relief from a discipline which we cannot exercise. (PAGE 25)
    G. A relief from knowing who will succeed a good man when he dies. (PAGE 26)

CONTENTS *(Continued)*

### IV. A DELIVERANCE FROM MANY GLOOMY FEARS. (Page 27)
A. There is no fear of disorder when Jesus has been making the disarrangement. (Page 27)
B. There is no fear of the devil among us because the Jesus keeps him out. (Page 28)
C. There is no fear that roots of bitterness should spring up among us. (Page 29)
D. There is no fear of our not being watered when Jesus undertakes to do it. (Page 29)

### V. A WARNING FOR THE CARELESS. (Page 30)
A. Those who are not planted by God should take heed. (Page 30)
B. The branches of the vine which bear no fruit should take heed. (Page 30)

### VI. IT IS A QUIETUS TO THOSE WHO COMPLAIN. (Page 31)
A. Those who suffer physical pain or temporal losses. (Page 31)
B. Those who have suffered bereavement. (Page 32)

### VII. AN OUTLOOK FOR THE HOPEFUL. (Page 33)
A. We may expect the best possible prosperity. (Page 33)
B. We may expect divine intercourse. (Page 34)
C. We expect he will remove the whole garden upward with himself. (Page 34)

# SUPPOSING HIM TO BE THE GARDENER

A SERMON BY

CHARLES H. SPURGEON

*Supposing him to be the gardener.*—JOHN 20:15 (KJV).

I was sitting about a fortnight[1] ago in a very lovely garden, among all kinds of flowers which were blooming in delightful abundance all around. Screening myself from the heat of the sun under the overhanging boughs of an olive, I saw palms and bananas, roses and camellias, oranges and aloes, lavender and heliotrope. The garden was full of color and beauty, perfume and fruitfulness. Surely the gardener, whoever he might be, who had framed, and fashioned, and kept in order that lovely spot, deserved great commendation. So I thought, and then it came to me to meditate on the church of God as a garden, and to suppose the Lord Jesus to be the gardener, and <u>then to think </u>of what would most assuredly happen

1  Fortnight—fourteen days; two weeks.

if it were so. "Supposing him to be the gardener," my mind conceived of a paradise where all sweet things flourish and all evil things are rooted up. If an ordinary worker had produced such beauty as I then saw and enjoyed on earth, what bounty and glory must surely be brought forth "supposing him to be the gardener"! You know the "him" to whom we refer, the ever-blessed Son or God, whom Mary Magdalene in our text mistook for the gardener. We will for once follow a saint in her mistaken track, and yet we shall find ourselves going in a right way. She was mistaken when she fell into "supposing him to be the gardener"; but if we are under his Spirit's teaching we shall not make a mistake if now we indulge ourselves in a quiet meditation on our ever-blessed Lord, "supposing him to be the gardener." It is not an unnatural supposition surely, for if we may truly sing

> "We are a garden walled around,
> Chosen and made peculiar ground,"[1]

that enclosure needs a gardener. Are we not all the plants of his right hand[2] planting? Do we not all need watering and tending by his constant and gracious care? He says, "I am the true vine, and my

---

1 A quote from *We Are a Garden Walled Around* by Isaac Watts.
2 Right hand—See Psalm 80:15.

Father is the gardener,"[1] and that is one view of it; but we may also sing, "My loved one had a vineyard on a fertile hillside. He dug it up and cleared it of stones and planted it with the choicest vines"[2]—that is to say, he acted as gardener to it. Thus has Isaiah taught us to sing a song of the Loved One touching his vineyard. We read of our Lord just now under these terms—"You who dwell in the gardens with friends in attendance, let me hear your voice."[3] To what purpose does he dwell in the vineyards but that he may see how the vines flourish and care for all the plants? The image, I say, is so far from being unnatural that it is most pregnant with suggestions and full of useful teaching. We are not going against the harmonies of nature when we are "supposing him to be the gardener."

Neither is the figure unscriptural; for in one of his own parables our Lord makes himself to be the man who took care of the vineyard. We read just now that parable so full of warning. When the "certain man" came in and saw the fig tree that it brought forth no fruit, he said to the person who took care of his vineyard, "Cut it down! Why should it use up the soil?"[4] Who was it that intervened between that profitless tree and the axe but our great Intercessor

---

[1] John 15:1 (NIV).
[2] Isaiah 5:1–2 (NIV).
[3] Song of Songs 8:13 (NIV).
[4] Luke 13:7 (NIV).

and Interposer? It is he who continually comes forward with "Leave it alone for one more year, and I'll dig around it and fertilize it."[1] In this case he himself takes on himself the character of the vineyard keeper, and we are not wrong in "supposing him to be the gardener."

If we would be supported by a type, our Lord takes the name of "the Second Adam," and the first Adam was a gardener. Moses tells us that the Lord God placed the man in the garden of Eden to work it and take care of it. Mankind at its best was not to live in this world in a paradise of indolent luxury, but in a garden of recompensed toil. Observe that the church is Christ's Eden, watered by the river of life, and so fertilized that all manner of fruits are brought forth to God. He, our second Adam, walks in this spiritual Eden to work it and take care of it, and so by a type we see that we are right in "supposing him to be the gardener." Thus also Solomon thought of him when he described the royal Bridegroom as going down with his spouse to the garden when the flowers appeared on the earth and the fig tree had put forth her green figs. He went out with his Loved One for the reservation of the gardens, saying, "Catch for us the foxes, the little foxes that ruin the vineyards, our vineyards that are in bloom."[2] Neither nature, nor Scripture,

---

1 Luke 13:8 (NIV).
2 Song of Songs 2:15 (NIV).

nor type, nor song forbids us to think of our adorable Lord Jesus as one that cares for the flowers and fruits of his church. We make no mistake when we speak of him, "supposing him to be the gardener." And so I sat quietly and considered the suggested line of thought, which I now repeat for you to hear, hoping that I may open many roads of meditation for your hearts also. I shall not attempt to think out such a subject thoroughly, but only to indicate in which direction you may look for a vein of precious ore.

I. "Supposing him to be the gardener," we have here THE KEY TO MANY WONDERS in the garden of his church. The first wonder is *that there should be a church at all in the world;* that there should be a garden blooming in the midst of this sterile waste. Upon a hard and flinty rock the Lord has made the Eden of his church to grow. How did it come to be—here an oasis of life in a desert of death? How did faith come in the midst of unbelief, and hope where all is servile fear, and love where hate abounds? "We know that we are children of God, and that the whole world is under the control of the evil one."[1] From what source is our being "of God" when all besides this is firmly under the control of the devil? How did there come to be a people for God, separated, and sanctified, and consecrated, and ordained to bring forth fruit unto his name?

1  1 John 5:19 (NIV).

Assuredly it could not have been so at all if the doing of it had been left to man. We understand its existence, "supposing him to be the gardener," but nothing else can account for it. He can cause the fir tree to flourish instead of the thorn, and the myrtle instead of the briar; but no one else can accomplish such a change. The garden in which I sat was made on the bare face of the rock, and almost all the earth of which its terraces were composed had been brought up there, from the shore below, by hard labor, and so on the rock a soil had been created. It was not by its own nature that the garden was found in such a place; but by skill and labor it had been formed—even so the church of God has had to be constructed by the Lord Jesus, who is the author as well as the perfecter of his garden. Painfully, with wounded hands, has he built each terrace, and fashioned each bed, and planted each plant. All the flowers have had to be watered with his bloody sweat, and watched by his tearful eyes— the nail-prints in his hands, and the wound in his side are the tokens of what it cost him to make a new Paradise. He has given his life for the life of every plant that is in the garden, and not one of them had been there on any other theory than "supposing him to be the gardener."

Besides, there is another wonder. *How did the church of God come to flourish in such a climate?* This present evil world is very uncongenial to the growth of grace, and the church is not able by herself alone to resist the evil influences which surround her. The church contains within itself elements which tend to its own disorder and destruction if left alone; even as the garden has present in its soil all the germs of a tangled thicket of weeds. The best church that Christ ever had on earth would within a few years apostatize from the truth if deserted by the Spirit of God. The world never helps the church; it is all in arms against it; there is nothing in the world's air or soil that can fertilize the church even to the least degree. How is it then that notwithstanding all this, the church is a fair garden unto God, and there are sweet spices grown in its beds, and lovely flowers are gathered by the divine hand from its borders? The continuance and prosperity of the church can only be accounted for by "supposing him to be the gardener." Almighty strength is put to the otherwise impossible work of sustaining a holy people among men; almighty wisdom exercises itself on this otherwise insuperable difficulty. Hear the word of the Lord, and learn from it the reason for the growth of his church below. "I, the LORD, watch over it; I water it continually. I guard it day and night so that no one may harm it."[1] That is the reason for the existence of a spiritual people still in the midst of a godless and perverse generation. This is the reason for an election of grace in the midst

---
[1] Isaiah 27:3 (NIV).

of surrounding vice, and worldliness, and unbelief. "Supposing him to be the gardener," I can see why there should be fruitfulness, and beauty, and sweetness even in the center of the wilderness of sin.

Another mystery is also cleared up by this supposition. *The wonder is that you and I should ever have been placed among the plants of the Lord.* Why are we allowed to grow in the garden of his grace? Why me, Lord? Why me? How is it that we have been kept there, and sustained in our barrenness, when he might long ago have said, "Cut it down! Why should it use up the soil?" Who else would have sustained such waywardness as ours? Who could have manifested such infinite patience? Who could have tended us with such care, and when the care was so ill-rewarded who would have renewed it so long from day to day, and persisted in designs of boundless love? Who could have done more for his vineyard? Who could or would have done so much? A mere mortal would have changed their good intent, provoked by our ingratitude. None but God could have had patience with some of us! That we have not long ago been slipped off as fruitless branches of the vine; that we are left still on the stem, in the hope that we may ultimately bring forth fruit, is a great marvel. I do not know how it is that we have been spared, except on this ground—"supposing him to be the gardener"—for Jesus is all gentleness and grace, so slow with his knife, so tardy with his axe, so hopeful that we would only show a bud or two, or, perchance, yield a little sour berry—so hopeful, I say, that these may be hopeful prognostics of something better in the future. Infinite patience! Immeasurable long-suffering! Where are you to be found accept in the breast of the Loved One? Surely the hoe has spared many of us simply and only because he who is meek and lowly in heart is the gardener.

Dear friends, there is one mercy with regard to this church which I have often had to thank God for, namely, that *evils should have been shut out for so long a time*. During the period in which we have been together as pastor and people, and that is now some twenty-nine years, we have enjoyed uninterrupted prosperity, going from strength to strength in the work of the Lord. Unfortunately we have seen many other churches that were quite as hopeful as our own torn with strife, brought low by declension, or overthrown by heresy! I hope we have not been apt to judge their faults severely; but we must be thankful for our own deliverance from the evils which have afflicted them. I do not know how it is that we have been kept together in love, helped to abound in labor, and enabled to be firm in the faith, unless it is that special grace has watched over us. We are full of faults; we have nothing to boast of; and yet no church has been more divinely favored. I wonder that the blessing should have lasted so long, and I cannot make it out except when I fall into "supposing him to be the gardener." I cannot trace our prosperity to the pastor, certainly; or even to my beloved friends the elders and deacons, or even to the best of you with your fervent love and holy zeal. I think it must be that Jesus has been the gardener, and he has shut the gate when I am afraid I have left it open. He has driven out the wild boar of the wood just when he had entered to root up the weaker plants. He must have been about at nights to keep off the prowling thieves, and he must have been here, too, in the midday heat to guard those of you who have prospered in worldly goods, from the glare of too bright a sun. Yes, he has been with us, blessed be his name! He is the reason for all this peace, unity, and enthusiasm. May we never grieve him so that he shall turn away from us; but rather let us invite him, saying, "Stay with us. You that dwell in the gardens, let this be one of the gardens in which you consider worthy to dwell in until the daybreak and the shadows flee away." So in these ways our supposition is a key to many wonders.

II. Let your imaginations run along with mine while I say that "supposing him to be the gardener" should be A SPUR TO MANY DUTIES.

*One of the duties of a Christian is joy.* That is a blessed religion which among its precepts commands people to be happy. When joy becomes a duty, who would wish to neglect it? Surely it must help every little plant to drink in the sunlight when it is whispered among the flowers that Jesus is the gardener. You say, "I am such a little plant; I do not grow well; I do not put forth much leafage, there are not as many flowers on me as on many around me!" It is quite right that you should think little of yourself—perhaps to droop your head is a part of your beauty—many flowers had not been half so lovely if they had not practiced the art of hanging their heads. But "supposing him to be the gardener," then he is as much a gardener to you as he is to the most lordly palm in the whole domain. In the Mentone[1] garden right before me grew the orange and the aloe, and others of the finer and more noticeable plants. But on a wall to my left grew common wallflowers and saxifrages,[2] and tiny herbs such as we find on our own rocky places. Now, the gardener had cared for all of these, little as well as great. In fact, there were hundreds of specimens of the most insignificant growths all duly labelled and described. The smallest saxifrage could say, "He is my gardener just as surely as he is the gardener of the Gloire de Dijon[3] or Marechal

1 Mentone—a city in southern France that Spurgeon enjoyed visiting. Dr. James Henry Bennet owned a wonderful eight acre garden in Mentone and helped to popularize the city as a resort spot for tuberculosis recovery.
2 Saxifrage—a perennial herb growing in crevices of rocks in mountainous regions.
3 Gloire de Dijon—a fragrant apricot-colored climbing rose.

Niel."[1] Feeble child of God, the Lord takes care of you! Your heavenly Father feeds ravens, and guides the flight of sparrows—should he not much more care for you, you of little faith? Little plants, you will grow healthy enough! Perhaps you are growing downward just now rather than upward. Remember that there are plants of which we value the underground root much more than we do the hull above ground. Perhaps it is not yours to grow very fast; you may be a slow-growing shrub by nature, and you would not be healthy if you were to run to wood.[2] Anyhow, let this be your joy, you are in the garden of the Lord, and, "supposing him to be the gardener," he will make the best of you. You cannot be in better hands.

Another *duty is that of valuing the Lord's presence and praying for it*. Whenever the Sabbath morning dawns, we should pray to our Loved One to come into his garden and eat his pleasant fruits. What can we do without him? All day long our cry should go up to him, "Lord, look over and visit this vine and the vineyard which your right hand has planted." We should strive desperately with him that he would come and manifest himself to us as he does not to the world. For what is a garden if the gardener never comes near it? What is the difference between it and the wilderness if he to whom

---
1 Marechal Niel—a large fragrant yellow rose.
2 Run to wood—grow well but without fruit.

it belongs never lifts up spade or pruning-hook on it? So that it is our necessity that we have Christ with us, "supposing him to be the gardener." It is our bliss that we have Christ walking between our beds and borders, watching every plant, training, tending, maturing all. "Supposing him to be the gardener," it is well, for from him is our fruit found. Divided from him we are nothing; only as he watches over us can we bring forth fruit. Let us be done with confidence in man, let us forego all attempts to supply facts of his spiritual presence by routine or rant, ritualism or rowdyism; but let us pray for our Lord to be ever present with us, and by that presence to make our garden grow.

"Supposing him to be the gardener," there is another duty, and that is, let each one of us *yield oneself up entirely to him.* A plant does not know how it should be treated; it knows not when it should be watered or when it should be kept dry—a fruit-tree is no judge of when it needs to be pruned, or dug around, or fertilized. The wit and wisdom of the garden lies not in the flowers and shrubs, but in the gardener. Now then, if you and I are here today with any self-will and carnal judgment about us, let us seek to lay it all aside that we may be absolutely at our Lord's disposal. You might not be willing to put yourself implicitly into the hand of any mere man (pity that you should); but surely, you, the plant of the Lord's right-hand planting, you may put yourself without a question into his dear hand. "Supposing him to be the gardener," you may well say, "I would neither have will, nor wish, nor wit, nor whim, nor way, but I would be as nothing in the gardener's hands, that he may be to me my wisdom and my all. Here, kind gardener, your poor plant bows itself to your hand; train me as you will." Depend on it, happiness lives next door to the spirit of complete acquiescence in the will of God, and it will be easy to exercise that perfect acquiescence when we suppose the Lord Jesus to be the gardener. If the Lord has done it; what has a saint to say? Dear afflicted one, the Lord has done it! Would you have it otherwise? No, aren't you thankful that it is even so, because it is the will of him in whose hand your life is, and in whose hand are all your ways? The duty of submission is very plain, "supposing him to be the gardener."

One more duty I would mention, though others suggest themselves. "Supposing him to be the gardener," then *let us bring forth fruit to him*. I do not address a people this morning who feel no care as to whether they serve God or not. I believe that most of you do desire to glorify God; for being saved by grace, you feel a holy ambition to show forth his praises who has called you out of darkness into his marvelous light. You wish to bring others to Christ, because you yourselves have been brought to life and liberty in him. Now, let this be a stimulus to your fruit-bearing, that Jesus is the gardener. Where you have brought forth a single cluster, bring forth a hundred! "supposing him to be the gardener." If he is to have the honor of it, then labor to do that which will give him great renown. If our spiritual state were to be attributed to ourselves, or to our minister, or to some of our fellow Christians; we might not feel that we were kindling a great necessity to be fruitful. But if Jesus is the gardener, and is to bear the blame or the honor of what we produce, then let us use up every drop of sap and strain every fiber, that to the greatest degree to which our manhood is capable, we may produce a fair reward for our Lord's travail. Under such tutorship and care we should become eminent scholars. Does Christ train us? Let us never cause the world to think lowly of our Master! Students feel that their *alma mater* deserves great things of them, so they labor to make their university renowned. And so, since Jesus is tutor and university to us, let us feel that we are bound to reflect credit on so great a teacher, on so divine a name. I do not know how to put it, but surely we should do something worthy of such a Lord. Each little flower in the garden of the Lord should wear its brightest hues, and poor forth its rarest perfume, because Jesus cares for it. The best of all possible good should be yielded by every plant in our Father's garden, supposing Jesus to the gardener. This much then on these two points—a key to many wonders, and a spur to many duties.

III. Thirdly, I have found in this supposition A RELIEF FROM CRUSHING RESPONSIBILITY. One has a work given them of God to do, and if they do it properly they cannot do it carelessly. The first thing when one awakes they ask, "How is the work prospering?" and the last thought at night is, "What can I do to fulfill my calling?" Sometimes the anxiety even troubles their dreams, and they sigh, "Lord, send prosperity now!" How is the garden prospering which we are set to tend? Are we brokenhearted because nothing appears to flourish? Is it a bad season? or is the soil lean and hungry? It is a very blessed relief to excessive care if we can fall into the habit of "supposing him to be the gardener."

If Jesus is the Master and Lord in all things it is not mine to keep all the church in order. I am not responsible for the growth of every Christian, or for every backslider's errors, or for every professor's faults of life. This burden must not lie on me so that I shall be crushed by it. "Supposing him to be the gardener," then the church enjoys a better oversight than mine; better care is taken of the garden than could be taken by the most vigilant watchers, even though by night the frost devoured them, and by day the heat. "Supposing him to be the gardener," then all must go well in the long run. He that keeps Israel does neither slumber nor sleep; we need not fret and despond. I beg you earnest workers, who are becoming depressed, to think this out a little. You see it is yours to work under the Lord Jesus; but it is not yours to take the anxiety of his office into your souls as though you were to bear his burdens. The under-gardener, the workman in the garden, needs not fret about the whole garden as though it were all left to them. No, no; let them not take too much on themselves. I implore you to bind your anxiety by the facts of the case. So you have a number of young people around you, and you are watching for their souls as they that must give account. This is well; but do not be worried and wearied; for after all the saving and the keeping of those souls is not in your hands, but it rests with one far more able than yourself. Just think that the Lord is the gardener. I know it is so in matters of providence. A certain man of God in troublous times became quite unable to do his duty because he laid to heart so much of the ills of the age. He became depressed and disturbed, and he went on board a vessel, wanting to leave the country, which was getting into such a state that he could no longer endure it. Then one said to him, Mr. Whitelock, are you the manager of the world? No, he was not quite that. "Did not God get on pretty well with it before you were born, and don't you think he will do very well with it when you are dead?" That reflection helped to relieve the good man's mind, and he went back to do his duty. I want you thus to perceive the limit of your responsibility—you are not the gardener himself; you are only one of the gardener's boys, set to run on errands, or to do a bit of digging, or to sweep the paths. The garden is well enough managed even though you are not head manager in it.

While this relieves us of anxiety it makes labor for Christ very sweet, because if the garden does not seem to repay us for our trouble we say to ourselves, "It is not, my garden after all. 'Supposing him to be the gardener,' I am quite willing to work on a barren piece of rock, or tie up an old withered bough, or dig a worthless sod; for, if it only pleases Jesus, the work is for that one sole reason profitable to the last degree. It is not mine to question the wisdom of my task, but to set about it in the name of my Master and Lord. 'Supposing him to be the gardener,' lifts the ponderous responsibility of it from me, and my work becomes pleasant and delightful."

In dealing with the souls of people, we meet with cases which are extremely difficult. Some people are so timid and fearful that you do not know how to comfort them; others are so fast and presumptuous that you hardly know how to help them. A few are so double-faced that you cannot understand them, and others so fickle that you cannot hold them. Some flowers puzzle the ordinary gardener—we meet with plants which are covered with prickles, and when you try to train them they wound the hand that would help them. These strange growths would make a great muddle for you if you were the gardener; but "supposing him to be the gardener," you have the happiness of being able to go to him constantly, saying, "Good Lord, I do not understand this singular creature; it is as odd a plant as I am myself. If only you would manage it, or tell me how. I have come to tell you of it."

Constantly our trouble is that we have so many plants to look after that we have not time to cultivate any one in the best manner, because we have fifty more all wanting attention at the time. Then before we are done with the watering-pot we have to fetch the hoe and the rake and the spade, and we are puzzled with these multitudinous cares, even as Paul was when he said, "I face daily the pressure of my concern for all the churches."[1] Then it is a blessed thing to do the little we can do and leave the rest to Jesus, "supposing him to be the gardener."

In the church of God there is a discipline which we cannot exercise. I do not think it is half so hard to exercise discipline as it is not to be able to exercise it when at the same time you feel that it should be done. The servants of the landowner were perplexed when they were told not to root up the weeds. "The owner's servants came to him and said, 'Sir, didn't you sow good seed in your field? Where then did the weeds come from?' 'An enemy did this,' he replied. The servants asked him, 'Do you

1  2 Corinthians 11:28 (NIV).

want us to go and pull them up?' 'No,' he answered, 'because while you are pulling the weeds, you may root up the wheat with them.'"[1] This afflicts the Christian minister when he must not remove a pestilent, hindering weed. Yes, but "supposing him to be the gardener," and it is his will to let that weed remain, what have you and I to do but to hold our peace? He has a discipline more sure and safe than ours, and in due time the weeds shall know it. In patience let us possess our souls.

And then again, there is that succession in the garden which we can not keep up. Plants will die down, and others must be put into their places or the garden will grow bare, but we know not where to find these fresh flowers. We say, "When that good man dies who will succeed him?" That is a question I have heard many times, until I am rather weary of it. Who is to follow such a man? Let us wait until he is gone and needs following. Why sell the man's coat when he can wear it himself? We are apt to think when this race of good brethren shall die of it that none will arise worthy to unloose the latchets of their shoes. Well friend, I could suppose a great many things, but this morning my text is, "Supposing him to be the gardener," and on that supposition I expect that the Lord has other plants in reserve which you have not yet seen, and these will exactly fit into our places when they become empty, and the Lord will

1 Matthew 13:27–29 (NIV).

keep up the true apostolical succession until the day or his second advent. In every time of darkness and dismay, when the heart sinks and the spirits decline, and we think it is all over with the church of God, let us fall back on this, "Supposing him to be the gardener," and expect to see greater and better things than these. We are at the end of *our* wits, but he is not at the beginning of his yet—we are nonplussed, but he never will be; therefore let us wait and be tranquil, "supposing him to be the gardener."

IV. Fourthly, I want you to notice that this supposition will give you A DELIVERANCE FROM MANY GLOOMY FEARS. I walked down the garden and I saw a place where all the path was strewn with leaves and broken branches and stones. I saw the earth on the flower-beds, tossed about, and roots lying quite out of the ground—all was in disorder. Had a dog been amusing himself? or had a mischievous child been at work? If so, it was a great pity. But no—in a minute or two I saw the gardener come back, and I perceived that he had been making all this disarrangement. He had been cutting, and digging, and hacking, and mess-making; and all for the good of the garden. It may be it has happened to some of you that you have been a good deal clipped lately, and in your domestic affairs things have not been in so fair a state as you could have wished—it may be in the church we have seen ill weeds plucked up, and barren branches lopped, so that everything is *en deshabille*.¹ Well, if the Lord has brought it about, gloomy fears are idle. "Supposing him to be the gardener," all is well.

As I was talking this over with my friend, I said to him—"Supposing him to be the gardener," then the serpent will have a bad time of it. Supposing Adam to be the gardener, then the *serpent* gets in and has a chat with his wife, and mischief comes of it; but supposing Jesus to be the gardener, misery to you serpent—there is a blow for your head within half a minute if you do but show yourself within the boundary. So if we are afraid that the devil should get in among us, let us always in prayer ask earnestly that there may be no space for the devil, because the Lord Jesus Christ fills all, and keeps out the adversary. Other creatures besides serpents intrude into gardens; caterpillars and palmerworms,² and all sorts of destroying creatures are apt to devour our churches. How can we keep them out? The highest wall cannot exclude them—there is no protection except one, and that is, "supposing him to be the gardener." Thus it is written, "'I will prevent pests from devouring your crops, and the vines in your fields will not cast their fruit,' says the Lord Almighty."³

---

1 Deshabille—a loose, negligent dress; a loose morning dress.
2 Palmerworm—any hairy caterpillar which appears in great numbers, devouring herbage.
3 Malachi 3:11 (NIV).

I am sometimes troubled by the question—What if roots of bitterness should spring up among us to trouble us? We are all such fallible creatures, supposing some brother should permit the seed of discord to grow in his bosom, then there may be a sister in whose heart the seeds will also spring up, and from her they will fly to another sister, and be blown about until brethren and sisters are all bearing rue and wormwood in their hearts. Who is to prevent this? Only the Lord Jesus by his Spirit. He can keep out this evil, "supposing him to the gardener." The root which bears wormwood will grow only a little where Jesus is. Dwell with us, Lord, as a church and people—by your Holy Spirit reside with us and in us, and never depart from us, and then no root of bitterness shall spring up to trouble us.

Then comes another fear. Suppose the living waters of God's Spirit should not come to water the garden, what then? We cannot make them flow, for the Spirit is a sovereign, and he flows where he pleases. But the Spirit of God will be in our garden, "supposing our Lord to be the gardener." There is no fear of our not being watered when Jesus undertakes to do it. "He will pour water on him that is thirsty, and floods upon the dry ground." But what if the sunlight of his love should not shine on the garden? If the fruits should never ripen, if there should be no peace, no joy in the Lord? That cannot happen "supposing him to be the gardener," for his face is the sun, and his countenance scatters those health-giving beams, and nurturing warmths, and perfecting influences which are needful for maturing the saints in all the sweetness of grace to the glory of God. So, "supposing him to be the gardener" at this the close of the year, I fling away my doubts and fears, and invite you who bear the church on your heart to do the same. It is all well with Christ's cause because it is in his own hands. He shall not fail nor be discouraged. The pleasure of the Lord shall prosper in his hands.

V. Fifthly, here is A WARNING FOR THE CARELESS, "supposing him to be the gardener." In this great congregation many are to the church what weeds are to a garden. They are not planted by God; they are not growing under his nurture, they are bringing forth no fruit to his glory. My dear friend, I have tried often to get at you, to impress you, but I cannot. Take heed for one of these days, "supposing him to be the gardener," he will reach you, and you shall know what that word means, "Every plant which my heavenly Father has not planted shall be rooted up." Take heed to yourselves, I pray.

Others among us are like the branches of the vine which bear no fruit. We have often spoken very sharply to these, speaking honest truth in unmistakable language, and yet we have not touched their consciences. But "supposing him to be the gardener," he will fulfill that sentence—"Every branch in me that does not bear fruit he takes away." He will get at you if we cannot. If only before this old year were quite dead, you would turn to the Lord with full purpose of heart; so that instead of being a weed you might become a choice flower; that instead of a dry stick, you might be a sappy, fruit-bearing branch of the vine. The Lord make it to be so; but if any here need the caution, I pray for them to take it to heart at once. "Supposing him to be the gardener," there will be no escaping from his eye; there will be no deliverance from his hand. As "His winnowing fork is in his hand to clear his threshing floor and to gather the wheat into his barn, but he will burn up the chaff with unquenchable fire,"[1] so he will thoroughly cleanse his garden and throw out every worthless thing.

VI. Another set of thoughts may well arise as A QUIETUS TO THOSE WHO COMPLAIN, "supposing him to be the gardener." Certain of us have been made to suffer much physical pain, which often bites into the spirits, and makes the heart to stoop. Others have suffered heavy temporal losses, having had no success in business, but on the contrary, having had to endure privation, perhaps even to penury. Are you ready to complain against the Lord for all this? I pray you do not do so. Take the supposition of the text into your mind this morning. The Lord has been pruning you sharply, cutting off

1 Luke 3:17 (NIV).

your best boughs, and you seem to be like a thing despised that is constantly tormented with the knife. Yes, but "supposing him to be the gardener," suppose that your loving Lord has brought it all about, that from his own hand all your grief has come, every cut, and every gash, and every slip—does not this alter the case? Has not the Lord done it? Well then, if it be so, put your finger to your lip and be quiet, until you are able from your heart to say, "The LORD gave and the LORD has taken away; may the name of the LORD be praised."[1] I am persuaded that the Lord has done nothing amiss to any one of his people. No child of his can rightly complain that they has been whipped with too much severity. No one branch of the vine can truthfully declare that it has been pruned with too sharp an edge. No, what the Lord has done is the best that could have been done, the very thing that you and I, if we could have possessed infinite wisdom and love, would have wished to have done. Therefore let us stop each thought of murmuring, and say, "The Lord has done it," and be glad.

Especially I speak to those who have suffered bereavement. I can hardly express to you how strange I feel at this moment when my sermon revives a memory so sweet dashed with such exceeding bitterness. I sat with my friend and secretary <u>in that garden</u> some fifteen days ago, and we were

1 Job 1:21 (NIV).

then in perfect health, rejoicing in the goodness of the Lord. We returned home, and within five days I was smitten with disabling pain; and worse, far worse than that, he was called on to lose his wife. We said to one another as we sat there reading the word of God and meditating, "How happy we are! Dare we think of being so happy? Is it necessary to quickly end it?" Little did I think I would have to say to him, "In sorrow my brother, you are brought very low, for the delight of your eyes is taken from you." But here is our comfort—the Lord has done it. The best rose in the garden is gone. Who has taken it? The gardener came this way and gathered it. He planted it and watched over it, and now he has taken it. Is not this most natural? Does anybody weep because of that? No, everybody knows that it is right, and according to the order of nature that he should come and gather the best in the garden. If you are sorely troubled by the loss of your beloved, still dry your grief by "supposing him to be the gardener." Kiss the hand that has brought you such grief? Beloved, remember the next time the Lord comes to your part of the garden, and he may do so within the next week, he will only gather his own flowers, and would you prevent his doing so even if you could?

VII. "Supposing him to be the gardener," then there is AN OUTLOOK FOR THE HOPEFUL. "Supposing him to be the gardener," then I expect to see in the garden where he works the best possible prosperity—I expect to see no flower dried up, no tree without fruit—I expect to see the richest, rarest fruit, with the daintiest bloom on it, daily presented to the great Owner of the garden. Let us expect that in this church, and pray for it. If we only have faith we shall see great things. It is our unbelief that straitens God. Let us believe great things from the work of Christ by his Spirit in the midst of his people's hearts, and we shall not be disappointed.

"Supposing him to be the gardener," then dear friends, we may expect divine intercourse of unspeakable preciousness. Go back to Eden for a minute. When Adam was the gardener, what happened? The Lord God walked in the garden in the cool of the day. But "supposing him to be the gardener," then we shall have the Lord God dwelling among us, and revealing himself in all the glory of his power, and the plenitude of his Fatherly heart; making us to know him, that we may be filled with all the fullness of God. What joy is this!

One other thought. "Supposing him to be the gardener," and God to come and walk among the trees of the garden, then I expect he will remove the whole of the garden upward with himself to fairer skies; for he rose, and his people must rise with him. I expect a blessed transplantation of all these flowers below to a clearer atmosphere above, away from all this smoke and fog and damp, up where the sun is never clouded, where flowers never wither, where fruits never decay. The glory we shall then enjoy up there on the hills of spices in the garden of God! "Supposing him to be the gardener" what a garden will he form above, and how shall you and I grow in there, developing beyond imagination. "What we will be has not yet been made known. But we know that when he appears, we shall be like him, for we shall see him as he is."[1] Since he is the author and finisher of our faith, to what perfection will he conduct us, and to what glory will he bring us! If only to be found in him! God grant we may be! To be plants in his garden, "Supposing him to be the gardener," is all the heaven we can desire.

---

1  1 John 3:2 (NIV).

# NOTES

# NOTES

# MAN'S QUESTIONS & GOD'S ANSWERS

**Am I accountable to God?**
*Each of us will give an account of himself to God.* Romans 14:12 (NIV).

**Has God seen all my ways?**
*Everything is uncovered and laid bare before the eyes of him to whom we must give account.* Hebrews 4:13 (NIV).

**Does he charge me with sin?**
*But the Scripture declares that the whole world is a prisoner of sin.* Galatians 3:22 (NIV).
*All have sinned and fall short of the glory of God.* Romans 3:23 (NIV).

**Will he punish sin?**
*The soul who sins is the one who will die.* Ezekiel 18:4 (NIV).
*For the wages of sin is death, but the gift of God is eternal life in Christ Jesus our Lord.* Romans 6:23 (NIV).

**Must I perish?**
*He is patient with you, not wanting anyone to perish, but everyone to come to repentance.* 2 Peter 3:9 (NIV).

**How can I escape?**
*Believe in the Lord Jesus, and you will be saved.* Acts 16:31 (NIV).

**Is he able to save me?**
*Therefore he is able to save completely those who come to God through him.* Hebrews 7:25 (NIV).

**Is he willing?**
*Christ Jesus came into the world to save sinners.* 1 Timothy 1:15 (NIV).

**Am I saved on believing?**
*Whoever believes in the Son has eternal life, but whoever rejects the Son will not see life, for God's wrath remains on him.* John 3:36 (NIV).

**Can I be saved now?**
*Now is the time of God's favor, now is the day of salvation.* 2 Corinthians 6:2 (NIV).

**As I am?**
*Whoever comes to me I will never drive away.* John 6:37 (NIV).

**Shall I not fall away?**
*Him who is able to keep you from falling.* Jude 1:24 (NIV).

**If saved, how should I live?**
*Those who live should no longer live for themselves but for him who died for them and was raised again.* 2 Corinthians 5:15 (NIV).

**What about death and eternity?**
*I am going there to prepare a place for you. I will come back and take you to be with me that you also may be where I am.* John 14:2-3 (NIV).

Printed in Great Britain
by Amazon